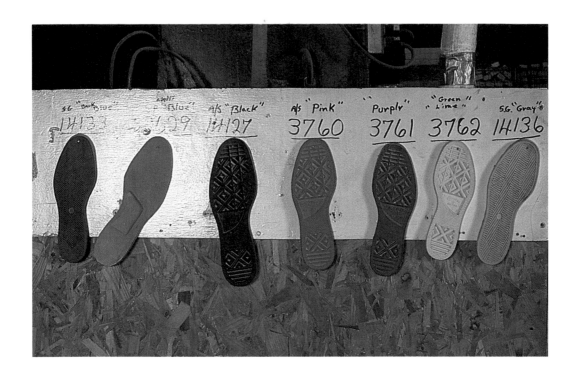

HOW ARE SNEAKERS MADE?

BY HENRY HORENSTEIN

SIMON & SCHUSTER BOOKS FOR YOUNG READERS
Published by Simon & Schuster
New York   London   Toronto   Sydney   Tokyo   Singapore

My special thanks to the many people who made this book happen, in particular Helene Fletcher, John Gniadek, and Jennifer Murray of Converse and all the people at the Converse factory in Lumberton, NC. Jim Dow lit up Converse. Valorie Fisher and Lawson Little helped make the cover photo work. Faith Hamlin and Sarah Olson of the Footwear Industries of America were very generous with their time. Thanks also to Frezzolini Severance Design, Westerly, RI; Pam Pollack, Lucille Chomowicz, and Theresa Gaffney at Simon & Schuster. And, as usual, Tracy Hill helped in too many ways to list.

SIMON & SCHUSTER BOOKS FOR YOUNG READERS
Simon & Schuster Building, Rockefeller Center,
1230 Avenue of the Americas, New York, New York 10020.

SIMON & SCHUSTER BOOKS FOR YOUNG READERS is a trademark of
Simon & Schuster.
Designed by Sylvia Frezzolini.
The text for this book was set in 14 point Baskerville.
Manufactured in the United States of America

10 9 8 7 6 5 4 3 2 1

Library of Congress Cataloging-in-Publication Data
Horenstein, Henry.   How are sneakers made?/by Henry Horenstein.
Summary: Describes the steps involved in manufacturing sneakers.
1. Sneakers—Juvenile literature. [1. Sneakers. 2. Shoes. 3. Shoe industry.] I. Title.
TS1017.H66   1993   685′.31—dc20
CIP   92–23811
ISBN 0–671–77747–5

This book is for Jim Dow,
the light doctor

It's hard to believe, but a hundred years ago sneakers didn't even exist. Today almost everyone wears sneakers. They are so popular that Americans spend more than five billion dollars on them every year. That's more than they spend on ice cream! You probably own a pair or two of sneakers yourself. But do you know how they are made?

To make sneakers, you need natural rubber. This comes from trees that grow in Malaysia, Indonesia, and other faraway tropical lands. The rubber is shipped to the sneaker factory in large wooden crates.

In a mill at the factory, rubber is mixed with clay, dyes, and chemicals to make it more durable and to give it color.

The rubber leaves the mill in long sheets and is stuffed into a machine called a cutter, which compresses the sheets into narrow strips.

Extruding generates a lot of heat—almost 200 degrees! The rubber must be cooled to keep it soft and flexible, so it is passed through a tank of water that has a temperature of 38° F.

The cooled strips then move through another cutter, which cuts them into rectangular blocks of rubber called slugs.

The slugs are then melted and shaped into outsoles—the bottom part of the sneaker—by a curing press. Molds that look like outsoles are loaded into the press according to sneaker size—from size 8 for babies to size 17 for basketball players.

A slug is positioned on top of each mold. The curing press is closed and heated to 310° F. The heat causes the slug to compress and fill the mold. In less than three minutes the outsoles are completely baked.

They are removed from the press in sheets.

The outsoles are then cut out of the sheets by an electric saw, and their rough edges are trimmed by hand. More than 4,320 outsoles, differing in style, color, and size, are produced daily by each curing press.

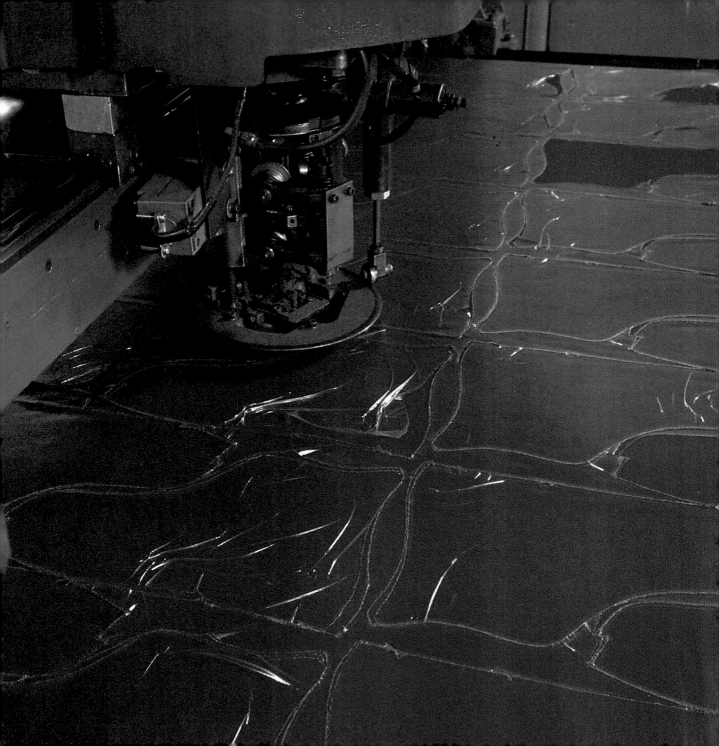

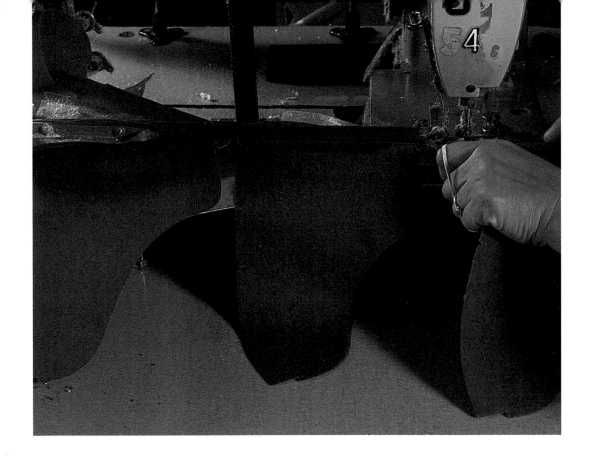

Meanwhile, in another part of the factory, a machine cuts out fabric for the uppers—the top part of the sneaker. A computer makes sure the correct number of uppers are cut.

The two sides of the uppers are sewn together with a heavy-duty sewing machine. First the machine attaches the sides to each other, then it stitches a fabric piece called a backstay over the seam where the sides are attached. The backstay strengthens the seam so the sneaker won't fall apart with wear.

High-top sneakers have ankle patches with the brand name on the inner side of each upper. The patches are applied by hand. Then a rotating table carries the uppers to a sealing station. At the station the patches are firmly bonded to the fabric.

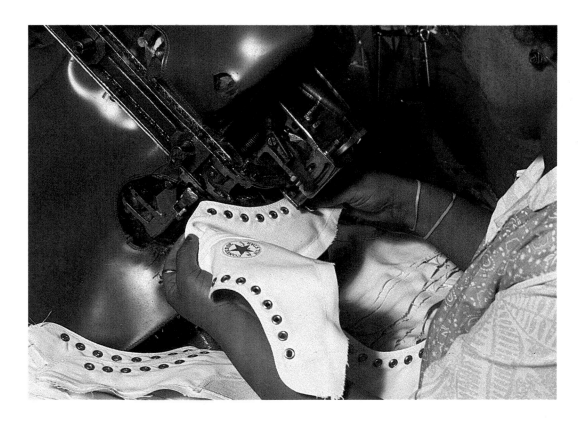

Eyelets with metal washers are then poked into the uppers. The washers add strength to the eyelets and keep the fabric from tearing when the laces are tied.

The finished uppers are hung on hooks until they are ready for assembly. They are sorted according to their size, style, color, and whether they fit the left or right foot.

The outsoles and uppers are now ready for final assembly on the making line. The line consists of a moving conveyor belt with workers sitting on each side of it. The workers add various parts until the sneaker is fully assembled. Several making lines run simultaneously, with each line producing four pairs of sneakers every minute!

Once an hour a count is made of each making line. This particular line started work at 7 A.M.; by 8 A.M. the workers had produced 246 pairs of sneakers. By 9 A.M. the total count jumped to 492—another 246 pairs. By 10 A.M. the count was 698. Only 206 pairs were made that hour because the workers took time out for coffee and doughnuts.

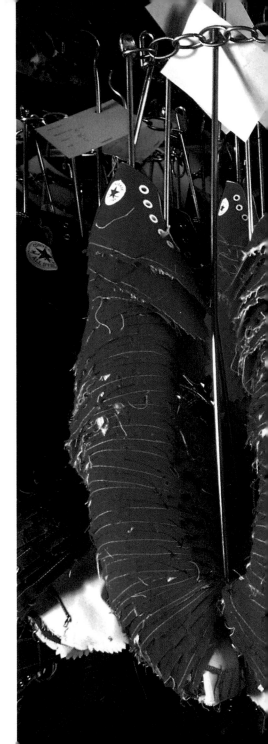

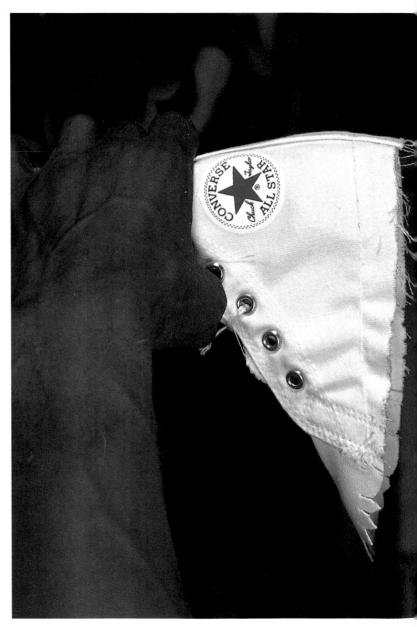

Each sneaker is assembled around a last, which is an aluminum mold shaped like a foot. Lasts are stored in baskets according to size, foot shape (left or right), and style.

While on a last, the upper is attached to the insole, a cushioned liner that protects the bottom of the foot. The upper and insole are glued together with a quick-drying cement.

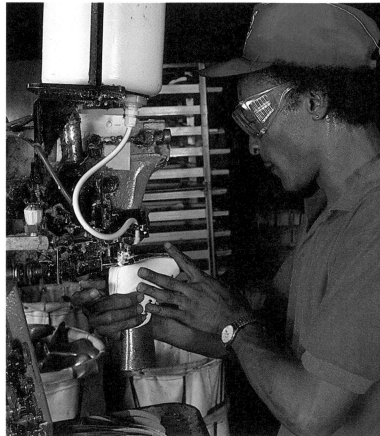

At the beginning of the making line, uppers and insoles are dipped into a gooey bath of rubber called latex. Other parts of the sneaker stick to the latex as these pieces are added.

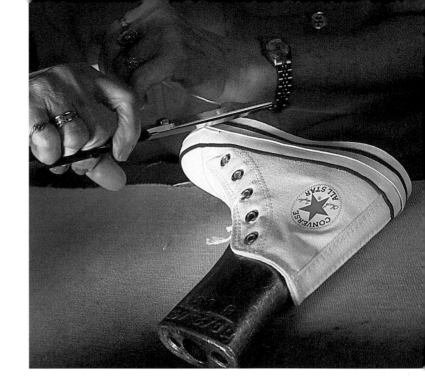

One of these parts is a strip of fabric called piping. The piping is coated with gum (a type of rubber, not something to chew). The piping is wrapped around the bottom of the sneaker, cut to fit, and then pressed in place with a roller.

Now the outsole is fitted under the insole, and a machine presses the two parts together tightly.

A bumper strip made of gum is glued to the front of the upper to protect the toe and to make the sneaker look good.

The sneaker passes through a set of rollers at the end of the making line. These rollers press all parts of the upper, insole, and outsole firmly together.

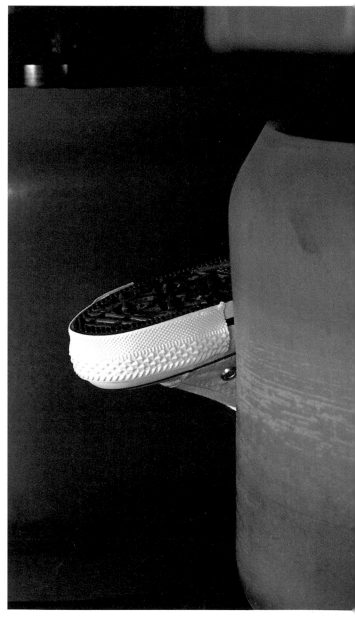

The brand label is glued to the heel of each finished sneaker. The sneaker is then placed in a hydraulic press, which squeezes the heel, toe, and sides together.

An inspector checks each sneaker and fixes minor defects. Mistakes are noted on a chalkboard according to the defective part. This way the mistakes can be traced and future problems can be corrected.

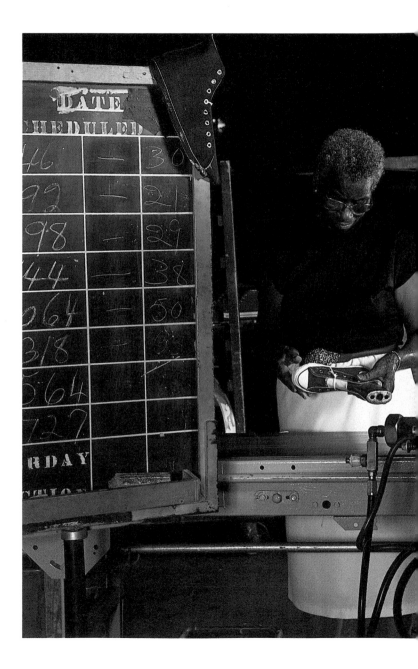

The sneakers are taken off the making line and placed on a rack. Each rack holds twenty-seven pairs. When twenty-one racks are filled, they are placed in a huge steel oven that is shaped like a tube. This oven is called a vulcanizer. It cures the sneakers by baking them for eighty-eight minutes at a temperature of 292° F. Curing helps give the sneakers strength and flexibility. When the time is up, the door opens automatically and the racks move out of the vulcanizer.

The sneakers are removed from the racks, taken off their lasts, and placed in plastic tubs according to size, color, and style. The tubs are delivered to the lacing and packing line by a series of conveyor belts.

Laces are looped through the eyelet holes so they won't get lost. More than fifty thousand pairs of laces are looped in this manner every day.

A machine punches eyelets with rivets in the inner side of each sneaker. These holes allow air to circulate, preserving the sneaker and keeping your feet from smelling.

Packing boxes are assembled by hand, and each pair of sneakers is wrapped in tissue paper. The wrapped sneakers are then boxed and packed in cases.

Each case contains twenty-four boxes of sneakers. The boxes are sealed, counted, recorded, and packed into the backs of trucks. The trucks take them to a central warehouse. From there they eventually will be sent to a store in your hometown.

Sneakers are amazingly sturdy, but sooner or later they wear out and need to be replaced. More than fifty million Americans will get a new pair of sneakers this year. Will you be one of them?